salmon35

American Paprika

PETER JOSEPH GLOVICZKI

Prose Poems

salmonpoetry

Published in 2016 by
Salmon Poetry
Cliffs of Moher, County Clare, Ireland
Website: www.salmonpoetry.com
Email: info@salmonpoetry.com

ISBN 978-1-910669-31-0

FRONT COVER ARTWORK: © *Maddy007* | *Dreamstime.com -*
Earth Globe On Black Photo

COVER DESIGN & TYPESETTING: *Siobhán Hutson*

Printed in Ireland by Sprint Print

Acknowledgements

The author wishes to thank the editors of the following publications, in which some of these poems first appeared:

2 River View "Paprika"

DMQ Review "Yearbook"

elimae "Run"

The Rochester (Minnesota) Post-Bulletin "Coffee," "How It Happened"

Contents

Paprika

There is a town in Hungary that is three miles away from the Austrian border. In the winter of 1956, mothers held hands with their sons and daughters and ran as fast as they could. When you asked where they were going, all they said was *away*. It didn't matter where they had been, that wasn't the point anymore. The point, as far as anyone actually knew, was to keep breathing. Husbands had gone into hiding, pressed a couple forints into their wives palms, and then went off to keep breathing. Now, it was up to the wives to keep breathing, too. Mothers, of course, had the added burden of making sure their kids kept breathing. So they ran, and to make sure they stayed together, they held hands.

Cracks

Mother do we have any bacon is a rather unusual question for a Saturday night. But it was a strange day. My grandmother took time out to tell me, in the dialect of the old country, that she was satisfied with the way I turned out. Neither a compliment nor a criticism, it was just a statement, one all her own. Years after she died, I learned she passed messages during the resistance, tucked them in a mailbox near the town square, always at noon on Thursdays. My grandmother did that for years, and I thought she was just a bitter seamstress.

Mortimer and My Mother

Mortimer was an invisible goat who lived under my bed. We both liked puzzles of tall buildings. We had almost nothing else in common. My mother accidentally killed him; she was vacuuming under my bed. I was in third grade when it happened and I cried, really cried, when she told me. My mother gave me Rocky Road, held me and said she was sorry. After twenty minutes, I forgave her: even mothers make mistakes.

The Atlas of Strange Places

I drew a map and called it good. There was
nothing to get up for, so I slept. Jackson
Browne was on the radio: I asked my father
for ginger ale money and I hit the road.

Yearbook

We drank lots of Dew Drop soda, drew up
maps in our heads and let the trees be our
guide: The squirrels always ran, ours was
small-town carnage about which I remember
little. Memory is a funny thing: The way
extremes get built up and corner our
hysteria; the way other things all melt. I've
forgotten Vivian Warnick, the way her face,
her blessed head, was a tiara built entirely to
rest upon her neck. How I wanted that neck
on Friday evenings, what we might've done,
restless and necking. She got lost in my
slideshow of bones and flesh. I painted my
room ivory, it was all I knew to rebel. I set a
radio by the bed, kept it on overnight and let
the hum tuck me in. It was 1974.

Elegy for the Only Way You Let Me Touch You

Across your back, my fingers swimming in tiny circles. I was sad because I thought this was something else. You knew better, and I should have: you always kept your clothes on—I never saw your flesh unkept.

August 2, 1979

I wanted a big red Cadillac, with a sofa seat in the back. Dad came home from work; we were going to pick it out. Then we heard Thurman Munson's plane went down. The newsman said he fell short of the runway. When Dad wasn't looking, I cried.

Equilibrium

The way I remember my brother is through his
black-and-white   photographs,   landscapes
mostly, that he took while on leave from here
to there or in-between and I have to wonder
these days where memory leads us: how the
weight of the past is light and heavy all at once.

Because the Night
Belongs to Lovers

I cut my right thumb on the edge of a granite
countertop. I was in someone else's kitchen;
Steely Dan was there, belting out their one
great song. And Laura Nyro, too, being *emo*
before it meant anything: I think her fingernails
were painted black, I didn't see her toes. There
was a small TV next to the sink; I reached to
turn it on and Patti Smith appeared.

Coffee

We met for coffee and talked about nothing
over onion rings; it was just what we needed.
Then we ordered curly fries and shared
Kennedy stories. I was on my 8th grade field
trip to the Science Museum. You were hanging
streamers in the high school gym before a pep
rally. We both cried when we heard the news. I
was in front of the dinosaur exhibit as I watched
the bones go blurry: you dropped a pair of
scissors and heard them hit the gym floor.

Love on a Cold Evening

My mother buys a standup light and sets it up
in the living room. Everything looks brighter:
it's Thanksgiving Day—I had turkey with my
girlfriend at her family's house. They live in a
college town; it's where I went to school. For
you, I'd name each star; the night sky would
light this room.

Afterlife Inventory

When her mother died, Sara snuck into her
Mom's bones. Moved into her old house;
wouldn't throw anything away. A shrine to her
shoes and belts and dressing gowns. A sanctuary
for her garden tools, her winter clothes. *That
stuff is just stuff*, she told me, *I need how the
floorboards creak. I don't feel heavy here*, she said. I
held her. A single light shone above the door.
And in the rain it flickered.

Boomer

When I was nine, my parents bought me a ferret: I named him Boomer. I trained Boomer to change the channels on the TV. He used his nose to do it—the two of us were featured in the local paper. Boomer became a celebrity. People came by, strangers rang the doorbell; they brought their own remotes. And Boomer was always up to the task. His nose got all the channels, even the illegal ones. When the cops found out, they took Boomer away. I told the cops to fuck off. That was the first time I ever swore.

Hungarian Waltz

We lined up in two rows: Boys facing girls, dressed to the nines. Your smile stole my knees while my belly ached. I learned a kind of pain that Fall; something that made the room hurt. And as our bodies danced around one another, I found the value of levitating flesh. It was a new age.

Name that Tune

In a café a woman sitting by the window reminds me of my mother.

I stare long enough to catch her eyes (hazel like my mother's) and I'm reminded of a song she used to love, a song she always played while cleaning the kitchen.

For a lazy Sunday, she'd say, singing words to a song I can't remember.

Jesse Lee

I know a woman with two black eyes. She was carrying a canoe above her head—holding up the front-end while I did the same with the back-end—and the damn thing fell on her. It was all my fault. I slipped on a slick spot in the gravel; it had just rained. The canoe left my grip and that startled her. Since then, I hold my morning coffee extra tight.

Creative Pastoral

While visiting an artist, I show him my sketches.

He tells me: *this one*.

This nose reminds me of something worth repeating.

Do this, he tells me, *five hundred times*—I gather my drawings and bring them home.

Drinks

I know a few poets who like to celebrate
Spring by getting drunk: they'll take any
excuse to buy a round of beers and shoot the
shit at the local bar. Who won which prize
recently, what famous young poet they'd bang
and how the world would be better if their
own poems were the ones getting all the best
press: I can't lie, wish I could, as I'm nodding
my head to them.

How It Happened

I met you with the bowl of oranges half-empty
on the kitchen table, light found your face
through the open window: the sun came to rest
in blue porcelain filling the bowl to its brim.

Crossing Over

It's my first fan letter and it comes on a Tuesday
full of bourbon and rain when even the dog's
looking at me funny as I kick off my boots and
stumble to the pile of mail you left with a note
that says *love you* and a pot of fresh coffee.

Florida, 1985

The shackles of February snow found my veins that year. I said *fuck this* to Sara and we packed it up. Found a cheap place on the sand and decamped. We were hungry; the locals said the main drag was the place to be. Joe DiMaggio was there. At the restaurant he loved, the back-table where nobody bugged him. *I guess everybody runs*, Sara said to me later, *the only question is from what*.

Photographs

Sara collects photographs of winter light at dawn. She's organized them into albums, placed chronologically on her favorite shelf: the top one in the sunroom that I built for her.

I'm no MacGyver, but my father gave me a hammer when I was young. Sometimes during foreplay, she'll ask for my favorite.

I've got the picture all picked out: November sun rising over the Mississippi; everything orange, even the snow, and the careful eye can see the reflection of the water in the corner of the shot. *I like what that one says*, I'll whisper, *how it doesn't need anything more.*

Pull

When we pulled our blood vessels up to our teeth, when we blew into them, they didn't make a sound. The aorta made rainwater noise against crisp leaves. There was no one else on the sidewalk.

Naming the First Child

You should feel free to select from the four names I have approved.

You should remember that I approved the names: Peter, Petra, Lauren and Jimmy.

You will want a name that communicates strength and power.

You will want a name that communicates grace and wisdom.

You will want a name that is both confident and humble.

You should feel free to disregard these rules when naming the first child.

You should keep them in mind when naming the second one.

Delivery

Luke was born on a Tuesday in April, at eight-fifteen in the evening; the surrounding buildings half-sunlit, half-shadowed.

You asked what I thought about my son.

I winced as you cradled him, left me frigid, wanting.

Everyday Litany

Simple things freak me out. Calling other people. Asking for a ride. Leaving the wrong number on an answering machine message. Giving bad directions. Forgetting to unplug the toaster, to turn off the stove. In conversation, spelling my last name phonetically. Spelling anything. A math problem. Long division. Where I'll be in ten minutes. A week. Ten years. Who I'll be with—whether you'll be there, too.

Make Yourself at Home

I won this TV in a poker bet with Steven Chase:
flopped a full house and beat his trip-nines.

I always watch the World Series of Poker on
ESPN and TIVO-it for Steven. I bought this
table at a furniture sale. When I asked about
the scratches the owner said his wife ran it
over with her car. *Better the table than you*, I
told him. He gave me a discount, threw in
some coasters I can't stand and shot me a
cock-eyed grin. Don't ask about the chair Sara
won at Bingo Night; that black leather beast
rules our living room. She's humming in the
kitchen, fixing lasagna, a modern Mayan
ritual. *Dinner*, she says, but actually an
offering for the chair. That beast talks
Descartes with the dog and, if I'm good, lets
me take a seat and watch TV. Wheel of
Fortune's on as I solve the puzzle: *I think
therefore I am.*

People With Kids

People with kids will talk about their kids. This is especially true among women under 30. Women under 30 will talk about their kids, you can count on that. Women under 30 will talk about what their son is doing in preschool. They will tell you about the foods he is, or is not, eating. They will tell you random things. Oranges will never seem so boring to you— neither will apples, bananas, or even the more adventurous fruits that you once, almost, considered trying. To be honest, people with kids will bitch about their kids. They will not bitch about their kids directly—no, that wouldn't be right—they will simply bitch about any number of things that their kids have done. This list may include, but is certainly not limited to: Painting on the walls, not wanting to wear pants and shouting *Fuck fuck* at random passersby. People with kids will bring in their son's drawing, or their daughter's finger-painting, and push-pin it up for everyone to see.

People with kids may, or may not, realize that their behavior tends towards the annoying and the slightly neurotic. This depends, quite frankly, on whether or not they are mindful of the world around them. If they are mindful of the world around them, you're in luck. In that case, they'll tell you a couple of self-involved stories about playing a newly-invented game—something involving kitchen utensils and socks, something that's played like basketball but scored like baseball, something like that. And then they'll laugh slightly, as if only to themselves—and say something almost sincere like *I'm sure you have work to do.* Be thankful if the people around you fall into this category. If they don't, then you're in trouble. People with kids who are not mindful of the world around them are, more or less, hopeless. They will talk and talk and talk and they will not shut up. They will never shut up. You can count on that, too. Trying to get these people to stop talking about their kids is like having an argument with a washing machine: It doesn't matter what you do—the spin cycle just keeps spinning.

The Truth about Cats and Dogs
(Or, How I Learned to Stop
Worrying and Love AC/DC)

I'm sorry, just really sorry, that I can't bring
your cat to the dry-cleaners with me: not
enough space in the hamper. You must
understand I operate within constraints, and
even if I didn't, she never liked me; she always
clawed me, flung sand in my general direction.
How would you feel in such a situation? Pets
are for people who dislike humans and need an
excuse to explain their aversion. I am a dog
person says the bumper sticker on the car in
front of me and I nod and smile at my car's
radio as AC/DC drives me home.

If You're in Benton, Kentucky

Write and tell me what it's like. I've been
frozen for twenty-six years amidst a gaggle of
Canadian geese. I hear them in my sleep.
Songbirds mean nothing to me; bright
mornings bring their lies by the fistful.

Kennedy Fantasy

You ask me and I think of the MTV VJ, the one
with the glasses, the first person I ever . . . .
And how I had her on TV, on the couch. That
afternoon everything went blue—cornflower
blue—stuck in the saccharin trap of the past:
good no matter how it hurt.

Nearby

I live next door to a man who trims bonsai trees. He's amassed quite the collection. At Christmas time, he puts one in each window. He makes sure they're facing North, though I'm not sure why. I'm in love with a woman who organizes her books based on their color. We met at a neighborhood party, where Neil gave a short talk about bonsai trees. I don't remember anything about it; I was too tipsy from drinking the hard apple cider.

Run

I stole your ankles the week before gas prices surged. Then I bartered them for this pair of lungs. It was bull. Bless the allure of their protective potential. Now, you'll track me down. You won't even blink. I'll need every breath here when you find me and I run.

Leslie

My niece told me she was comfortable with
her legs open; I dropped the ice cream on the
linoleum floor.

The dog was pleased, but I sure as hell wasn't:
Leslie told me she'd been taking pole-dancing
classes—*for fitness*, she insisted.

You're thinking about it all wrong, she
continued, in the way only 17-year-olds can;
*I'm doing this to please myself, and I'm comfortable
with my legs open.*

Well I'm not, I thundered back; and we stood in
the kitchen watching each other as the dog
licked ice cream off the floor.

Cosmopolitan Dream

The weight of a half-empty cup in my left hand after dark; just the moon and Billy Joel on the keys as a passing siren out my open bedroom window reminds me why I moved to the city.

All-American Barbeque

They've minimized the bullshit associated with eating out. There's nothing perfect, nothing pristine. Sauce smeared on the table. I'm glad to lay my sleeve down; I don't like to eat alone.

Near Prescott, Wisconsin

We're miles from anywhere when you call to beg me back.

We're in a one-bar town on the Wisconsin border.

Leslie and I are downing *the coldest beer in town*.

She grabs my cell and hands it to the bartender.

Don't give this back to him, she says.

He nods at her and fills my mug.

The Listener Speaks

I admit to quitting too quickly for my own taste. This confession will kick you square in the crotch. I wish I had a softer way to fashion it, but I'm from the Midwest—never learned to fight clean or dirty, and I don't hang around for make-up beers. I'm always en-route to somewhere. The distance to my destination constant: languishing forever between a rock and a cornfield, one vainly awaiting a plow. I am not the man for the job, but I'll listen while you tell me who is: even I get tired of nothing.

The Gift

Last night I licked the salt out of my wounds
and called it a victory.

I remember when I lost my way: I let go slips
of paper to mark the path, so I wouldn't take
that road again.

Won't you come visit me love, we could drink
wine: you and me.

I stopped writing letters when the price of
stamps went up.

You wrapped my gift in newsprint; in the
comics.

Due Diligence

The door swings open funny, and it doesn't close.

The window creaks when the cold gets at it.

Look out for sharp edges on these bookshelves.

The kitchen is simple, but newly-remodeled.

Stainless-steel appliances. Granite countertops.

Up the stairs, you'll find a small guest room.

Here's a shower and a half-bath, great for company.

I hope you like the place; stay and look around.

If you have any questions, my number's on the card.

The Water in March

I read about a man whose body was found
floating in the Hudson River. I don't know
how it happened; I'm from Minnesota, we
have 10,000 lakes, one river: the Mississippi.
No one swims in it, which is to say they
shouldn't. People do. I knew a guy once; he
drowned. It was an accident. The current. The
water in March was still chilly.

In the Wind

There is a kind of stop-loss policy on faith
after a while. Put another way, faith ends.

I watch women tossing coins into the fountain
in the center of town.

I like to wait for a splash. The way ripples off
water know to make a circle.

The way the breeze turns flowers into acts of
geometry: tease me, lover, tease me.

The City (Rain and Fireflies)

The city is the same grey today as it was yesterday.

That fact is its own kind of simple comfort. Exhale.

I dreamt of fireflies: eleven of them above my bed.

The water will get two inches deep on my flat roof.

But it didn't rain yesterday, the sky was just grey—

I like to hold on to that color, a particular comfort.

There is a song in my head about fireflies. Fireflies.

I can't hear them in the deep water on my flat roof.

Worth

Someone I went to high school with has just asked to be my *Facebook* friend. This does not surprise me. In his profile picture, he is holding a giant fish of some sort, also no surprise. The fish is splayed out and surely dead; a kind of Midwestern conquest—a modest way of saying look, here is what I can do, what I am worth.

Elegy for the Scraps

Elvis taught me about sex; all-night radio did the rest. Imagine a time before you remember; picture yourself in that void. My bones like that place, confusion and all. Rust surrounds most of my childhood; not good or bad just misremembered, unremembered, as if wiped entirely from the record. Here's what I know; scraps come back every now and then: the kind that stay with you, the kind you can't forget.

Stash

I found my Christmas money, fresh bills,
between pages 42 and 43 of a book I've
never read. The bills were resting in the
middle, not sticking out the top. When I
closed the book—when I held it shut—the
money disappeared.

Look Before You Leap

You come to know a man by the facial
expressions of his family members in a
Christmas portrait. Smiles might suggest the
calendar flew by. Stoic expressions carry the
weight of work. My kin is a gallery 300-
million-strong. Alive in America, in the world-
at-large, like the dancing girl and high-wire
man: known to measure each and every step.

Distance

And the harpist lets her fingers speak

*

Listeners clap through their gloves

*

Lovers force half-smiles

*

Lips climb each side of the glass door

*

Even the voyeur, staring, backs away

You Asked Why I Don't Get Out Much

I slit a man's throat with a kitchen knife. I snuck up behind him on a slippery street, in December; the year the Vikings bought Moss. A few paces away, I asked for the time. When he turned to answer, I went to work. I hid the body in the dumpster behind Subway. I paid Adam Monberg eight hundred bucks to get rid of the guy, and haven't seen Adam or the body since.

Calendar Days

I don't feel different this new year but truth
follows me all the way to work, wagging its
wiry tail while I sing a song I learned by heart
before I fell from grace and power, which are
the same salvation dressed differently.

Seeking New Coordinates

Found a map of America in the attic. Brought
it downstairs. Made room on the kitchen
table. Spread out to find a country new to me.
Funny what happens, once you know where
you've been.

Sunday Evening

It's late. I've got one leg in my briefs and I've put on my sleep shirt. On the other side of this wall, someone is playing guitar. Or piano. There's music from another room.

Photograph by Karen Kloser.

PETER JOSEPH GLOVICZKI is a teacher, a communication researcher and a poet. His poems have appeared in *Hayden's Ferry Review, New Orleans Review, The Christian Science Monitor, Verse Daily* and elsewhere. *American Paprika* is his second book of poems. He is also the author of *Kicking Gravity* (Salmon Poetry, 2013). He works as an assistant professor of communication at Coker College in Hartsville, South Carolina, where he also serves as coordinator of the communication program. His first scholarly book is *Journalism and Memorialization in the Age of Social Media* (Palgrave Macmillan, 2015). His scholarly journal articles have appeared or are forthcoming in *Health Communication, Humanity and Society, Journal of Loss and Trauma* and *The Qualitative Report*. He holds a PhD and an MA in Mass Communication from the University of Minnesota, and he is a magna cum laude graduate of St. Olaf College in Northfield, Minnesota.